Joy's War

Published by
Roscoe, Wilmott, Boothman &
Associates

© 1998-2014 JEK Clark (Story), RWB &
Associates (Design)

Joy's War

The Tale of a Nurse and Her Soldier

Dedication

To my Mum and my sister Josephine Case.

J E K CLARK

Foreword

"I feel I'm living in a legend," is how my sister felt about Mum's stories. As children we were brought up with them. My favourite was the one about Vesuvius. She would sit for hours and tell you all about her adventures during the Second World War. She wrote a diary and kept it by her bedside. I loved the stories and felt it was important to share them. Ordinary lives lived in exceptional situations. One can almost feel the comradeship, the excitement as well as sensing the danger and seriousness of what was going on in those years. Mum's obvious sense of humour pervades her writing, and carries the reader through.

Her diary records a brief moment in time, but what a time!

Mum was a strong character and had always been a lively, determined person.

However, she was willing to laugh at life and see the funny side of things. Mum's stories were as much a part of her as everything else. They made up who she was. Reading the diary in its entirety for the first time had quite an impact on me. All the stories that I'd grown up with and appreciated had their own individuality. Now, I have a context and that makes them all the more vivid and alive. It opened up a part of her life that I knew little about. I feel I have lived through it with her. It is important that these memories are not forgotten and can be passed on to the next generation. Once our elderly relatives are gone, those memories and experiences are lost forever. Unless we capture them before it is too late.

Mum was born on the 24th May, 1919. I always remember her birth year because I had a penny, in 'old money', with 1919 stamped on it. She was christened Dorothy Joyce Barber, but everyone knew her as Joy. Her parents had wanted her christened Joy, but were not allowed, as it was not looked upon as a 'proper' name. She grew up in Kent, and was the eldest of four children. She had two brothers and a sister. Her father owned a nursery, and grew produce for Covent Garden. The house, 'Rosedale', was named after a dale found in the North York moors where her parents had spent a holiday.

There were four nurseries along that particular stretch of road. The greenhouses were 200 yards long and as children, it was great fun (and also very risky) to run along the plank between the greenhouses. I remember doing it once. There were the packing sheds as well. Highly skilled women would carefully pack the produce.

Mum remembers the drays leaving in the early hours of the morning to catch the markets. The London markets were particularly fussy. Ferns were grown all the year round, but there were also tomatoes, cucumbers, lettuce, phlox and large blooms of chrysanthemum. Sometimes, when there were extra flowers, bunches would be brought indoors. Their heavy scent would permeate throughout the house. Her father had come back from the First World War, a war hero. Tall, dark and handsome, he had lied about his age when he joined up, so he was quite young. He volunteered to go 'over the top' in the dead of night, and cut the wires, ready for the advance at daybreak. It was extremely dangerous. He was awarded the DCM – Distinguished Conduct Medal. He was only about eighteen.

Mum remembers a picture of Vesuvius hanging on the wall at her granny's house. Granny Barber lived next door and the sitting room at the front of the house was never used, except for special occasions. The picture of Vesuvius hung there. Little did mum know that one day she would see the volcano for real and be caught up in its devastating power.

Mum was a Queen Alexandra nurse during the war, known as a QA. Nursing required four years in training which she started at the Kent & Sussex Hospital, Royal Tunbridge Wells. During the war as a QA, her rank was automatically Captain. She followed the 1st army setting up field hospitals. Her hospital was the 103. She was often referred to as 'Sister Sunshine', as she was always cheerful and smiling.

She met Tony Case, who was my sister's father, whilst working on the wards. He was a patient with a broken leg due to a motorbike accident. He was a lively patient, and she was 'warned to take care' by interfering father! The following are extracts from her personal diary. Some of the details are as she told them to me as stories, and some are taken from her diary.

This is her story.

England 1942

Summer 1942
Back in theatre. Visits from Tony - on crutches! Persistent young man. Have to admit, very attractive. Tony discharged to convalesce. Visits continue and becoming serious.

Tony back with his Unit stationed locally. Frequent meetings - Sevenoaks - London. Even took him home to meet the family. Whoops!

Matron offered me post of sister on E.N.T. (ear nose and throat) wards and theatre but had already decided to volunteer for

Military Service.

<u>Nov 1942</u>

Joined Queen Alexandra's Imperial Military Nursing Service, Reserves (QAIMNS/R).

First posting, Leeds Castle near Maidstone, an officer's hospital.

<u>Leeds Castle</u>

Living in a castle quite an experience. Part supposedly haunted. Very noisy at night due to the peacocks! Beyond the drawbridge, a sentry on duty - to ward off intruders?! My friend Scotty convinced some ghosts thereabouts in the ruins beyond the 'moat'.

Unaware had an admirer - Tank Reg Padre visiting the sick. Patients joked it was me, not them, he came to see! Finally accepted Padre's invitation to dinner, Maidstone Hotel. My carriage was what appeared to be a baby tank! (later told a scout car). Embarrassed to have a proposal of marriage - oh dear! Said I was already engaged - sort of!

Tony very attentive, am much attracted - is this love?!

<u>*Weekend leave with Tony in London.*</u>
Saw 'Road to Morocco' starring Bob Hope and Bing Crosby. We decided to make

part of the film our 'code' to know where we were as I also would shortly be going overseas. Was three months at Leeds Castle.

<u>*Second posting to Netley Hospital.*</u>
Mobilising for Overseas Service began. Not issued with tropical kit so we think N. Africa. Tony already there.

<u>*13th March 1943*</u>
Arrived in the middle of the night in blackout train (had no idea where we were going!) at Avonmouth, Bristol. Sailed on a hospital ship called 'HMHS Newfoundland'.

It happened to be the very same ship

that Mum's cousin, Charles Antlett, had been on as a scout when he sailed to Australia. The HMHS Newfoundland was later torpedoed near Salerno during the invasion.

As we left the docks were cheered on our way by dockers. Only 12 QAs on board.

Because of mine fields in the Bristol Channel, sailed round the top of Ireland, into the teeth of a force 10 gale.
Busy destroyer warning us off convoy.

She told me that their ship was all lit-up like a Christmas tree, because it was a hospital ship. However, it kept getting mixed up with the convoy, as they had trouble controlling the now-empty ship. A small destroyer kept signalling them to keep away, as the convoy was meant to be travelling in darkness.

Gibraltar 1943

<u>18th March Gibraltar</u>
'The Rock' looked sheer & impressive and bristling with unseen guns. The bay was filled with navy shipping of every kind; Rodney, Nelson, Battleships, Destroyers and Corvettes…

Vivid blue sky and sea, blazing sunshine, multi-coloured distant hills – abundance of wild spring flowers and … BANANAS!! Small boats buzzing around offering them to us, not seen at home for four years.

<u>Evening</u>
Myriads of lights shining on

'The Rock' and across the water in Spanish Morocco.

<u>Night</u>
We are anchored in this harbour surrounded by other ships of the navy. Black velvet sky, the swish of water against the side of the ship - safe after our violent journey, through the Bay of Biscay, calm after the storm.

<u>19th March Morning</u>
Such a welcome, invitations galore to visit other ships - Matron unwilling to let us go! However, some 'high up' Naval Commander persuaded her we would be safe!!! Parties ++, men, men and more men - but we

must be properly escorted by Naval Officers! Laughter and fun.

Held up for 2 weeks because of u-boat activity in the Med. A large convoy had been attacked.

There were apparently QAs stationed permanently at Gibraltar, but nobody had ever seen them. It was a standing joke that they were afraid to come out because of all the men!

Poor Little Patience
Mum had told me about a time when she was attending lip reading classes in Wells. She said that she had made quite a few friends, one of them being Francis, who made her laugh a lot, and had a terrific sense of humour. Most of the class were of a particular age, and had lived through the war years. One day, Mum was sitting between 'poor little

Patience', who was 81, three years younger than herself and Francis. Apparently, Patience had been a Wren during the war, and was sent to Gibraltar.

"I was sent to Gibraltar in 1943. When were you there?" Mum asked her.
"1944," says Patience.
"Did you enjoy it?"
"Oh no," says Patience. "It was awful," she says with a very straight face. "I was only 18, and my parents hadn't told me anything."

Mum said that she was aware of Francis gently shaking with suppressed laughter at her side. She had told me Patience was a vicar's daughter and had clearly led a sheltered life. She said Patience had continued with the same very straight face, talking about the men. Here, Mum searches for Patience's exact words.

"They wanted so much."

At this point, Francis couldn't contain herself any longer & burst out laughing. When I asked mum about her time in Gibraltar, she had replied, "I had the time of my life."

But I add not in that sort of way, it was the social life that Mum enjoyed.

North Africa

28th March

Sailed up the med to Algiers. Sad farewell beneath the stars. From the deck watched the twinkling lights of Gibraltor disappear. Sunny peaceful days in the Med, lay on the deck all day eating oranges and almonds. One 'Jerry' plane came and took a look at us. It was announced that everyone was to go up on deck so that the plane could see nurses etc were on board. Red crosses ablaze. He went away - bit scary though.

31st March Algiers

Dazzling white buildings

shining in the morning sun. Palm trees.

Our men, doctors and orderlies welcoming us at the dockside but they were dressed in odds & ends, and looked a real mess, a bit untidy!

"Is this how you dress for active service?" someone called out. The answer that came back was that they had been torpedoed, and lost most of their gear. Only one orderly was lost. A lot of equipment had been lost including the padre's record collection.

<u>*Journey to Guyotville*</u>

Our men go ahead to find suitable area for field

hospital. Sisters went to Transit Camp. Dusty white road. Arabs in picturesque ragged costumes, brilliant colours and bearded (rather frightening) faces, filthy barefooted children, veiled cowed women.

<u>Transit camp</u>
Gay, luxury white villas on a headland, rocky, beautiful coastline, brilliant blue sea, white crested waves breaking at our feet. Tent for our 'Mess' - our first taste of canvas living! Using our camp kit in empty villas, trouble with beds! Fortunately our batmen dealt with this problem. Sort of holiday - lazed on the rocks and

silver sand in next bay.

<u>3rd April</u>
Dispatch rider brought message - Tony wounded and in 94th G Base Hospital in Algiers! Amid great excitement, Frances and I hitched a lift in army jeep to Algiers and out to 'Beni Messous' - became daily occurrence, starting after breakfast, returning for supper.

Tony suggests we get married!! Wow, I am staggered - could we? How? Apply for permission to marry from our Colonels. I have to tell and ask Miss Bloore (matron). She's shocked and not very helpful. However Colonel delighted. Some 'holdup' (took 3 months) question asked in Houses of Parliament, N. Africa being a foreign country and a war zone. In due course, permission granted.

<u>15th April Leave for Mecha Chateaudun</u>
Terrible train journey, 36 hours through mountainous desert country, no sign of life, bleak and barren. Intense heat, flies and dust. Black smuts from engine - shortage of water. Slept! On stretchers, choked by smoke, bumped and bruised.
Arrived exhausted, filthy and thirsty! Ambulances

'race' train to 'station', loud cheers as we climb down - our 'workmates', doctors and orderlies very pleased to see us and anxious to make us welcome.

Darkness falling, bumpy ride to 'hospital' - immense rocky field, SAND! 'planted' with tents - rocky, semi-mountainous 'hills' around, no trees, no other sign of vegetation - could be the surface of the moon?? Where are we? Apparently on a plateau, some miles from Constantine. Bitterly cold nights despite intense daytime heat.
WORK next morning equipping 'wards' - 4 large,

24-bedded tents. Me as Medical 1 with Capt. Brod and 4 orderlies plus 1 Staff Sgt. and 2 clerks (privates), to help with clerical work and keeping general good order! Capt. Brod, my boss, was Czechoslovakian.

No patients yet - our side not very busy.

<u>Living Quarters</u>
Sisters' lines somewhat removed from male staff lines?! We have large mess tent equipped with own chef and batmen/orderlies. Our sleeping tents are I.P.s. Indian Pattern - in 2 lines, and we share 2 to a tent. The loos are on the far horizon or so it seems if

you're in a hurry! 4 seated per side with canvas screens between the 'holes'! Food pretty basic and in short supply - I like corned beef!

Living under canvass put Mum off camping for life and hence as a child, we never went camping.

The Field hospital, No 103, sited close to the railway line, single track, with passing spaces, which runs across top of N. Africa, hugging coast few miles inland. Patients boarded on ambulance train from Front Line Dressing Station. Our hospital is half-way to Base Hospital, Algiers. Our job, as train stops, was to take off the more urgent cases for treatment - others went on to Base.

Slight hitch before we could start taking patients... sudden tropical RAIN - duration 3 weeks! Colonel had been informed that rainy season over! Ho! Ho! Camp awash with slippery, sandy mud. Colonel puts us into <u>male</u> battledress and army boots - quite lethal - I fell into a ditch (helpfully dug by R.E. (Royal Engineer) unit to drain the camp site).

Throughout her life, Mum was never comfortable wearing trousers. I remember she did not approve of my sister and I wearing trousers into town, but that soon changed. She was, after all, of a generation that felt you were not properly dressed unless you had matching shoes, handbag and gloves.

I was rescued by my Staff Sgt. Skinner - very wet, muddy and terrified - I want to go home! This life not for me - seems I have fallen at the 1ˢᵗ hurdle! However, with great care, taken into the Clerk's tent and plied with very strong sweet tea - cure for all ills in a sticky situation. Staff Sgt. Skinner forty years +, regular army, deemed too old for fighting unit, transferred to R.A.M.C. (Royal Army Medical Corps). As such, knows full well how to cope when stationed in wild and unfriendly situations.

<u>*Brewing up...*</u>
British Army - salt of the

Earth. Interesting how they 'Brew Up' as it's called.
Washed out petrol can.
Packet or 2 STRONG TEA.
Milk - condensed
Water to fill can.
Fire. Gather stones to make fireplace - set alight. Bob's your Uncle! The result in my case simply foul, but I had to accept their concern for me, and their kindness with good grace, and profuse thanks. I think we will make a good team.

My Nursing Orderlies also 'friendly' and fairly well trained in Basic Nursing. GDO bottom of the pack - empty the slops and bins, carry water containers from the Cook House - you name *it. My GDO named Bailly. We have been in action for a while now, large numbers of acute cases. Prepare large tent ward in hurry, all hands on deck - grabbed Bailly, although not a Nursing Orderly - could teach him as we go along - no need, he knew. Why? He said he had been a hospital porter!*

"Why didn't you tell them?"

"They didn't ask!"

Must get him to take the training exams on offer - will increase his pay and allowance to his wife. He was chuffed, said he'd like that.

Tony still at convalescent hospital, daily letters - very chirpy.

June

Days of intense heat, but nights very cold. Blazing relentless sun, no shade, bare rock, no green, nothing grows!

Sirocco fierce wind blowing off the desert, sand storms every day - sand everywhere, eat it, drink it, in our clothes, in our beds! The sand gets into everything and sticks to you. The wind drops with sundown, but is there again in the morning.

Constantine

Small party, doctors, sisters got together and arranged trip to Constantine in borrowed ambulance!

Amazing city built by the Romans on two mountain tops - bridges connecting the two sections. Meal in Officers' Mess - sort of palace taken over by the Army.

<u>*Night Duty*</u>
Different team, but find I still have my Senior Nursing Orderly and Bailly - appears they asked for the move to stay in my team. Sleep very difficult, dust, flies, lizards. We sleep NUDE under our mosquito nets. Our Batmen bang noisily on our tent poles to wake us up before appearing with our tea! Time to grab a sheet.

FIRE

Sgt. Major organized group to burn dried up vegetation (fire hazard) around camp, presumably to create a fire barrier! Went wrong, got out of control, caught alight the last tent in our night staff lines. Shouting woke me up - mine 3rd tent down, able to get out and collapse it, a method we had been shown to do in such an emergency - grabbed clothes and RAN! Amazed to find Tony had arrived, and outside our Mess in some panic! Draped in a sheet, covered in sweat and sand - assured him I am OK, except for blisters on hands. The fire under control, two tents totally *lost, four girls lost all their kit. United with my trusty tin trunk. R.S.M. for Court Marshal! Tony had flown up from Algiers, able to stay weekend. Blissful.*

<u>Day Duty</u>
Back with Capt. Brod, my old team and faithful Bailly, now happily getting upgraded to Nursing Orderly 2nd class.

I love the way Bailly features in Mum's diary. He was often there in the background, helping out and giving support. She claimed that he was not her batman, but he often took on the role of one. She always spoke very highly of him, and they obviously made a good team.

Malaria season and Dysentery. Stong winds - sand storms every day.

Two more flying visits from Tony. Wedding arrangements settled!! My 'leave' arranged, given my travel warrant and the blessings of my Colonel. Feeling very excited and can hardly believe this is going to happen.

<u>*30th July*</u>

Board 'Rapide' (plush 1st class carriage) for Algiers. Misnomer, not really fast at all, except that it does the journey in one day. Single track but at intervals, passing places. Hectic, sweaty journey, in company with four other male officers (not from our unit). Arrive <u>four hours late</u>. Frantic Tony on platform. Happy, happy reunion.

<u>31st July</u>
Married in the British Consulate by the Consul, also had religious marriage service in English Church in Algiers. Had spent the night (alone) in strange 'Arabian Nights' type hotel. Got lost trying to find a restaurant for breakfast. Tony arrived early to rescue me with taxi, off to the Consulate, driven by a hunchback.

- could be lucky -
Carved splendid marble staircase, hand in hand

and laughing happily, ascended. We forgot needed two witnesses! The Consul greeted us and laughed at our lack of insight, and summoned two clerks to do the job! An official piece of paper declaring us truly married. Congratulations all round and many good wishes.

Off in same taxi to the English Church.

<u>*English Church*</u>
Here met by various friends Tony has accumulated while being in hospital and convalescence - good at this sort of thing. Fatherly Maj. Lynn Harris to give me away and Tony's Captain

friend to be the best man. Huge bouquet of flowers.

Reception
Reception in apartment owned by Viscount Corvedale, Tony met him in Officer's Club, heard of forth coming marriage, and insisted on playing host to celebrations. Large gathering, a few QAs from 94th Base Hospital - didn't know a soul. Champagne ++ photos, silly speeches! Great fun.
Left for luncheon - wedding breakfast. Party of ten guests. I was the only woman - can't remember what we ate! We slip away quietly, and wander around the town in

something of a haze, and thinking we were on cloud nine.

<u>Honeymoon in Chenoua Plage</u>

Nine days heaven in almost paradise! We arrived in time for dinner, followed by a dance. Lt. Col. in charge arranged a big celebration party including getting an orchestra. Convalesced patients, doctors, sisters, all known to Tony, or most of them. I was overwhelmed.

Whenever it was seen that we were dancing together, the orchestra played the Anniversary Waltz.

This was a beautiful French

holiday resort - white villas, blue and green shutters. Verandahs covered in vines, colourful creepers, shady trees, figs - rocky beautiful coastline, golden sands. Moonlight bathing in the cove. Introduced to playing poker! Some French still here, a café still functioning. Dinner under the trees, café on the cliff. Watched big yellow moon rise out of the sea. Hitched one trip into Algiers, looked at the shops - pretty bare. Casbah out of bounds - looked and smelled interesting. Pity not allowed in.

<u>8th August</u>
End of holiday. Back to

Algiers for one day. Went to a sort of night club, naval types all over the place - several Destroyers in harbour, invited onto one of them for hectic party - their relaxation between sorties in the Med.

<u>9th August</u>
Up at 6.30am to catch 'Rapide'. Travel together, me to 103, Tony back to his unit somewhere on front line. Sad journey back. We got very dirty from soot, very hot and tired. Slept most of the way. Bailed out at 103 Gen. Hospital - Tony put up in Officer's Mess for night - not allowed to be with me!

10th August

Tony goes off to join his unit, me, duty on med ward. More Sirocco, heat and flies. Work ++

German patients

Back with Capt. Brod. Unfortunately two wards now full of German patients. This was because Brod was the only doctor to speak German. They are well behaved, but surly. Some fighting amongst themselves, so Brod separated the non-Nazis from the more militant types.

Day Duty

After the American Air Force arrive, there was one

particular German patient who would look under the folded-back 'tent walls' and count the American 'Flying Fortresses' going out in the morning. He would take great delight in counting them when they came back, to see if any were missing.

Some of the Germans very aggressive, and maintain they <u>will</u> win the war!

<u>Night Duty</u>
Two wards of prisoners. Only <u>one sentry</u> - rather frightening. However, no trouble.

<u>September</u>
R.A.T.D. arrive! Royal Artillery Training Depot.

Tented camp almost on our doorstep. Hostilities over in N. Africa, easing of restrictions, fewer patients, mostly medical.

Our chef prides himself on his ability with low and uninteresting rations, and with Matron's permission, would like to serve old fashioned 'Afternoon Teas' on Sundays. We thought it a great idea and it worked. So successful, word got about, not only our own officers begging for an invitation, but somehow the news got to the R.A. Depot. Every Sunday our mess was the most popular place on the planet!

A visitor

I was writing up notes in my office tent when a young Sgt. came in. I didn't look up.

"Yes?" I said.

He didn't say anything and just stood there. When I finally looked up, all I could see was this huge grin under his cap. Heavens it's Freddie! (one of Mum's brothers). He was with the 8th Army but Fighting was over. He hitched through the 1st Army lines searching for the 103 hospital and found me. We collapsed in laughter and embraces. We had two happy days talking, talking!!

Joy's War

Mum and Freddie were very close in age. They did everything together and most people thought they were twins. Freddie lives in Australia, and came to visit England in 2014 (the first time he has been back to the country in over two decades). Like Mum, he is full of stories. Freddie was busy chatting away to various members of the family in another part of the house, when I remember my cousin coming into the room and exclaiming, "Dad's on about the war again!" He told me a lot about his childhood and about some of the things, he and Mum would get up to. This is just one of those things:

<u>The Clock Incident</u>
Mother & Father played tennis. They would leave Joy in charge of Rex (the little brother). If the kids got too noisy Granny, who lived next door, would bang on the kitchen wall. One game Freddie & Joy would play was 'chasing'. This involved opening a window downstairs and the two windows onto

the balcony. It wasn't a real balcony as there were no doors, a 'show piece' as Freddie called it. The kids would climb in and out of the windows, much to the alarm of the neighbour across the road, who could see all this happening!

Rex was meant to go to bed at 7 o'clock, but sometimes he would get in the way, so they tried to put him to bed earlier. The problem was that Father had taught him how to read the Roman numerals on the clock and he would point at the clock and say, "But it's not 7 o'clock yet!" So Joy & Freddie came up with a plan. Joy would take Rex out of the room on some false pretence, leaving Freddie to climb up and change the hands on the clock. When Rex was safely in bed, Freddie would then have to put the hands back to the right time, but he didn't always get it right. Years and years later the truth came out.

"I wondered why that clock was playing up!" said Father.

Chatting to Freddie, I asked him if he had ever smoked, this was his reply, "I gave it up when I was 9 years old! " He said with a twinkle in his eye. "I tried one of Father's pipes and didn't like it!"

Freddie loved horses and would spend hours down at the local stables. When he joined up, he wanted to join the Cavalry. "Sorry mate." he was told. "No cavalry in this war!"
So he joined the artillery instead.

E.N.S.A. Concert
Rather rude - but went down well with the patients and our male staff.

Two women from YMCA arrived to cheer us all up! They persuaded the R.E.s to erect canvas screens around small area of tables and chairs creating what we are pleased to call the

'Hula Hula' and these two wonderful ladies produced 'teas', scones and things but mainly wonderful dishes with melon which along with dates seem to be infiltrating from outer space! Obviously more food stuffs coming on the railway instead of ammunition for front line.

<u>American Air Force arrives!</u>
Flying Fortresses - bombing Pantelleria and Sicily ready for invasion of Italy. Quickly found our camp close by and becoming a big nuisance. Very generous with their better rations - all sorts of wonderful food in tins. However, there is a price to pay. They haunt our

mess and continually invite us to their camp. Their idea of relaxation between their bombing raids is two-day drunken parties. I attend one (famous band leaders and big band) but never again!

Hospital fairly slack - we have a lot more free time. I do extra night duty. Worried about Tony. His unit part of the invasion of Italy.

<u>*October*</u>
Tony arrives in big convoy, sick and wounded from Italy - Salerno Landings. Visit frequently - progress slow but is winning. Not allowed up and I can't cart

him off to the 'Hula Hula'. A party of us visit Constantine, Tony more or less convalescent but must take care <u>not to drink alcohol</u>. I don't think he did, but he certainly seems a bit high and someone dared him to climb the statue in the middle of square opposite the Officers' Club. Huge female figure with enormous breasts - of course he <u>did</u> and sat on a breast - cheered on by the crowd now gathered!! Tony pronounced fit and discharged to I.R.T.D. (Incident Response Training Department) at Phillipvile.

Miss Blore, our matron, sent home, unfit for duty - she hasn't been well all the time we've been here, too old for Active Service.

Awaiting replacement, another TAN (Territorial Army Nurse) I expect. Unfortunately they are too 'old school' for this sort of job.

<u>*28th Oct*</u>
Begin closing down the hospital - great excitement. Where next?! Weather getting bad, COLD and some rain.

Before saying farewell to the desert, the tents and the everlasting SAND, flies, lizards - camping is <u>out</u> for me forever - here are some amusing incidents I have not so far recorded.

One blistering hot day about noon, standing with Staff Skinner and Bailly outside my office tent, we were amazed to see a startling sight. Suddenly there appeared a large caravan of camels and sundry dark-clothed Arabs moving slowly and with definite purpose straight through the middle of our camp from one end to the other. Not a word was said, not a sound was made that we heard. Don't know whether they were accosted by the Sgt. Major at the other end, think not. They

Kent & Sussex Hospital Staff Nurse 1942

Joy 1944

Tony & Joy (Algiers) 1943

HMHS Newfoundland

Tony in uniform

Leeds Castle

Kent & Sussex Hospital, Tunbridge Wells

Royal Victoria Military Hospital, Netley

Gibraltar

Algiers

Chenoua Plage

Bay of Naples

Washing very primative, Canvas basin for everything body or clothes.

Tony & Joy Case (Italy) 1944

Tony Case (Bari) 1946

Frederick Barber 1918

Joy, Jo, Freddie, Rex, Eileen, Bertha & Frederick 1948

Joy & Angus

were a formidable sight. Appears we had inadvertently pitched our tents on an ancient track used over hundreds of years across the desert, and no way would they change their route for a few tents!

Another incident we thought very funny at the time but our Seniors did not, was soon after we arrived on the plain. Major Huff Wuff complained of thieving from his stores - tins of course, but also spare mosquito nets. He was inclined to think some of the orderlies were flogging them in Constantine rumoured to fetch £5 a net. Arab ladies were making them into dresses due to the nets being made of silk. One of our officers claimed to have seen some garments in a shop in Constantine looking suspiciously as if made from mosquito nets!!

As for the food going missing, Huff Wuff at a bit of a loss but concluded 'Arabs' were getting in at night unseen and unheard by the sentries! So he came up with a brilliant idea - single wire around stores, knee height, attach numerous empty tin cans. The noise was horrendous in the middle of the night.

1ˢᵗ Nov

'Leave' to Constantine with Tony, seven days. If he gets 'leave', I am also given 'leave' automatically, with my colonel's good wishes. I am to meet Tony in Constantine. An ambulance going that way so I get a lift. A truck overturns on the way there, just in front of our ambulance, officer killed, and two others injured. Take them back to 31ˢᵗ General.

Arrive at the Casino in Constantine two hours late - Tony getting desperate! We had a little room at top of Transit Hotel which was once the 'Grand Hotel', now taken over by army. Very happy week. We had lots of fun, and explored the ancient and marvellous town. Dinner every night at the Casino, listening to the orchestra and watching people - remember the blond violinist, and the funny little man who played the cello. Flashily dressed Arabs - obviously very rich - some French Officers in splendid uniforms. What unit? Must be attached to the Arabs! They looked as if they had escaped from an Edwardian Musical Comedy!

Tony had a cold, which I caught of course and dampened our last two days. However, it was all absolutely marvellous - so much in love with each other - it's heaven.

<u>8th Nov Back to Chateaudun</u>
Feeling rather miserable. Reported back to Miss Simpson, our new matron, TAN and fortyish. She arrived last week. Of course, she didn't know me, and seemed very surprised that I had been on leave. Not only surprised, but outraged! I felt a distinct feeling of unfriendliness, obviously hadn't been told of my absence. Explained the situation, husband on leave so I got leave. She certainly didn't approve of such 'goings on'. Of course,

in her day, nurses didn't marry. If they did, they left!! Not a good beginning.

Bitterly cold nights, and daytime getting cold too. No patients now, nothing to do. A series of farewell dinners with our R.A.T.D. friends and we still have our makeshift dance floor. Great news, Mary has become engaged to Peter, our dentist. His persistence has paid off. He got promptly posted to a Base Hospital, can't have lovers together in the same unit!

Packing up continues. There's nothing for us to do, all work done by our orderlies.

Two huge store tents close to our lines, full of camp beds and blankets. Two orderlies sleep in each tent supposedly looking after contents. We woke this morning to find the tents and contents had disappeared but the orderlies were sleeping peacefully where the tents had been! Hadn't heard a thing. The Major, our Quarter master, hopping mad!

Got news, Tony back in hospital 100th Base Hospital Phillipville, abscess on bottom!

<u>26th Nov We move to Phillipville</u>

Horrid, bumpy, long, cold journey, though got much warmer as we came off the plain, and reached the sea. Several of us go to the 100th in transit, what luck.

Tony allowed up, and can leave the hospital but must be back on his ward by nightfall! And of course, I have to be in a different part! However, we have some glorious days by the sea - very happy again. Go to the Officers' Club for dinner and dancing every night. Go shopping and buy a lot of dates, melons and oranges. We have our favourite, special place on *the sand to eat them, and have taken to reading aloud to each other.*

12th Dec Reflections
We sat in our usual place today and talked a little about the future. Now I'm back in our temporary quarters, sort of dormitory, Tony gone back to his ward.

At another crossroads.
Looking back on these extraordinary and eventful months, can hardly believe so much has happened so quickly. Last Autumn began our whirlwind romance. Joined the Q.A., posting to Leeds Castle, Christmas... No way did I think I would be married before the next

one! Posting to severely bombed Southampton Netley Hospital - no patients but a centre for mobilisation for overseas. All the time, almost daily letters, wonderful letters from Tony always declaring his love for me - then they stopped for a while. This meant only one thing - he must have left the country - where? But I soon know, our 'code' worked! And at last I had an address for him - North Africa - 1st Army.

That cold February at Netley, miserable place, and uncertain of the future. Tony's love letters were a great solace. I have them all. Don't laugh at me as I *know you will when you read this. You wanted me to keep a diary. It isn't exactly that, but I have recorded what thoughts might amuse one day.*

My arrival in Algiers to find you wounded and in a Base Hospital with a broken leg in plaster and other nasty wounds, recovery likely to be a long job, you deemed it to be a bonus, the fates decreeing we should cement our love for each other and marry forthwith. We are so young yet the war has made us so much older than our years.

And so to the desert and our Field Hospital; some ghastly days, some funny days, some only just bearable days! But thank goodness for a sense of humour and some very good friends.

And so we get married. Tony back to his unit, training for the next move the war will take. We have the odd leave together, blissfully happy. Who knows what tomorrow will bring? With it all you remain optimistic, so sure we have a happy future ahead in a calmer world.

Now another parting looms tomorrow as the next day I shall be gone to Italy, leaving you to finish your convalesce and then back to your unit somewhere in Italy too. Light awfully bad in this place, better find my bed.

<u>*13th Dec we sail for Italy*</u>
HMS Dorsetshire, rather old and shabby, whole unit on board. As the sun sets we leave the harbour, my friend Mary and I standing together by the rail watching the lights on the coast grow dim, thinking of Peter and Tony sadly watching us go. Rough crossing, lots of people sick - fortunately I'm a good sailor.

Italy 1943

<u>16th Dec 1943 Naples</u>
7am sailing into the breathtaking beauty of the Bay of Naples, sea calm now and the sun shining brightly but then as we get closer, we notice that the harbour is littered with damaged ships, the buildings behind in ruins. Impossible for ship to dock properly, gets as close as possible. Ropes are fixed across and we had to clamber over upturned ships' bottoms (!) clinging to the ropes - very slippery, very scary! Helped up onto the dockside, man-handled really! However, we got there and found several

ambulances waiting to transport us further. Drove away through crowds of people shouting and throwing flowers at us. What a welcome!

Hectic drive through battle-scared streets, damaged buildings all around. Long bumpy drive out into rural countryside. Arrive at Castellamare - Transit 'camp'. Huge impressive building. We are told that it was once a famous palace - could have fooled me! Later it became a renowned hotel. During German occupation used as hospital for wounded. Building now badly damaged. Situated half way up a mountainside and proved to be overrun by RATS, fleas and bugs of all description. Drainage and water system nil and you wouldn't believe the PONG!! This apparently was the best on offer as a temporary lodging while our men folk set off to scan the countryside for a suitable place to be our hospital. They tell us it has to be in a special area with access to something that is about to occur!

<u>The stove</u>
We were given a very large smelly room on the top floor, bleak and bare, with broken shutters at the windows. The only items of

furniture are four iron beds with very suspect mattresses. In the middle of the room is a large, iron, wood-burning stove, chimney going up through the ceiling, NOT alright and very dirty. Our bed rolls arrived - very damp. Unfortunately getting luggage off the ship had understandably been somewhat difficult and a few things got dropped in the water - had certainly touched it!! We looked around in dismay. It was bitterly cold - something must be done about that STOVE.

"Let's explore". I suggested. We found plenty of trees

and woody undergrowth in what must once have been the 'grounds'. We gathered as much kindling and logs and bits that we could carry back to our garret. Mair, the practical one, always carries a goodly amount of toilet rolls, essential luggage, now to prove their worth in another way. While others watched in trepidation, I stuffed a quantity of toilet roll paper into the stove, followed by kindling and matches. Hey Presto! We had warmth. Very popular with all our other friends, "Please show us how to do it," they said.

No bathrooms, no running water, had to collect one pint each in biscuit tins from downstairs, had to do for everything. Had our cook with us and a couple of orderlies. Food very basic, mainly bully beef. We were often reduced to drinking hot water with marmite mixed in.

Although bitterly cold and snow higher up the mountains, we had marvelous walks through the forest, scrambling along goat tracks. Gather firewood - rule of the house, never go walking without coming back with a bundle of wood!

Not long before the word

got out and we were visited (and indeed rescued) by R.A. officers from nearby Battery. Better food and added bonus, TRANSPORT! Got to Naples or what's left of it, very badly bombed.

Army taken over one fairly decent building, must have been a 'posh' hotel, now a pretty good Officers' Club. Our new friends managed to organise a couple of rather hectic parties.

<u>*Christmas Eve*</u>
All rather homesick. Decorate our room, drew funny pictures on the walls.

Collected evergreens and stuff that looked like holly.

Got invited and escorted to dance at Officers' Con. Home in Sorrento.

<u>Christmas Day</u>
In better spirits. After lunch at R.A. Mess served 'tea' to the 'lads' on lovely green site amid cheers and shouts of joy. Back in mess for dinner, everything laid on. Where did they get it?? Dance and concert afterwards.

<u>Boxing Day</u>
Big post in today, stacks of letters from Tony. Dinner again with R.A. friends. Another party, another dance!

30th December
Super dance at the Officers' Con. Home at Sorrento, had a marvelous time - feeling a bit guilty knowing Tony working hard - retraining and getting ready to rejoin his unit. I seem to be having all the fun, but it can't last.

New Year's Eve
What a day, rained buckets and we move to Nocera to open our hospital.

Nocera
Dreadful buildings - ex-Barracks, leaking roof, what's left of them, half the windows missing, broken shutters, no lights, no heating and no water in

the taps. Local population had sheltered in it during fighting and left all their mess behind. Retreating Germans had blown up mains and sewer. We surveyed it all in horror. Told it must be ready to receive patients in two weeks!

<u>New Year's Day</u>
We begin work! Orderlies marvelous. R.E. did wonders to restore basic lighting and plumbing . We swept out the muck and disinfected everything! Very busy throughout January, convoys of wounded plus, plus. Some really bad cases. Working on B2 surgical and have my faithful Bailly

back, now Nursing Orderly 1st class, always by my side. We work long hours but better to have something to do again. To his delight, Tony sent back to Algiers, but think it's only temporary.

Things settle down. Our 'Mess' quite decent now cleaned up. Food has improved slightly, plenty of fruit and wonders of wonders, cauliflowers galore!

Getting some off duty now, the odd party and dinners at the Officers' Club in Naples. When having lunch at Officers' Club in Naples with Francis, crowded dining room, was asked by head waiter, could two other officers share our table? Of course! It was a Colonel Prodgers and his Adjutant! We were somewhat taken back. However, they proved very pleasant and chatty, rather friendly in fact. Col. offered to drive us back to Nocera in his staff car - arrived back in state - a few raised eyebrows!

<u>*Mid January*</u>
Hospital busy but getting regular off duty. Col. Prodgers in touch - I seem to have made a hit in high quarters!

Took me to Amalfi, very beautiful marvelous drive around the coast, sensational views, staff car and driver. A few days later, Col. Prodgers sent message inviting me to accompany him to a dance in Salerno. When we got there, I was very surprised to find we were the guests of honour! And worse - embarrassed to find Matron there - way down the table! Oh dear!

<u>4th February Night Duty</u>
Leaving the mess I am not surprised to find Bailly waiting outside to carry my bag. He always manages to make the change with me. I don't ask but I am very

grateful that he chooses to work with me.

As we walk across the Barrack Square to our ward block, Vesuvius looms large and menacing, large flames and sparks reaching into the sky. Bailly casts a wary eye and gruffly announces, "That's going to blow up one of these days sister!"
I laughed and said, "No! It's safe enough, been like that for hundreds of years."

Happy, happy reunion, two days together. Tony has acquired a flat in village. We discuss our future plans in some depth. Tony has decided he wants to stay in the army. They are already seeking out the young men who will form the basis of the Regular Peacetime Army and he wants to be part of this. He sees our future based on what he is learning and training for now. Tony goes back to Naples for War Office Board and passes out in highest grade for a Regular Commission. Tony goes to I.R.T.D. north of Naples - very, very busy.

<u>Time for Reflection</u>
Those few days we had before Tony left and we talked about our future and how the war was going, victories in Italy as the allies force their way up

the centre of Italy. Tony knows his unit is up to something special – not telling me exactly of course.

Things hotting up at home – hundreds of American Troops massing in England, obviously getting ready for an invasion of France. Letters from home full of it, and not all complementary to the U.S.A.! One or two of my patients express concern, wives telling of rowdy parties, nylons as gifts, how the Yanks have money to burn! I try to ease their worries, since their wives wouldn't write about it if they had anything to hide!

Mum said that they were very pleased to have the Americans, as they brought a lot of manpower and much needed equipment. But she also said that many of them were young and inexperienced compared to our men who had already gone through a lot.

I digress. We feel strongly and hopeful that the war will soon be over. Tony very optimistic and he also thinks he will soon be upgraded to Captain - more money - we do so want to start a family - shall we go for it? The time seems right.

Night duty progresses fairly quietly. These very fit, tough, mostly young men recover from their wounds quickly and especially as we have this magic new drug, penicillin. Have been told we are the first hospital to try it out.

Mum said the results were miraculous. They had never seen anything like it before. Wounds that used to take a long time to heal, now suddenly healed very rapidly.

It just so happens that I know the daughter of the boy who was one of the first civilians treated with penicillin in the United Kingdom. This is his account.

<u>John's Story</u>
John Hayter was 10 years old when, one day in 1943, while playing 'tip it and run' at Hanworth School, Middlesex the air raid siren went off. In the following few minutes in the pushing and shoving of trying to get 40 young children to the safety of the air raid shelter, John was kicked on his left foot. There was no time to clean the wound properly at the time and no more thought was given to it. However, a few weeks later, John was

experiencing serious pain and inflammation in his injured foot. He was taken to visit his doctor, whose response was that John was suffering from 'growing pains'.

Within a few days John's whole leg was inflamed and he was admitted to Ward D2, (The Childrens Ward) of Staines Emergency County Hospital London, which had been set up to deal with the overflow of casualties from the London bombings. On arrival at the hospital John's consultant, Mr Woodwalker, was unsure of a diagnosis. It was another doctor, who on sight of John's X ray, diagnosed Osteomyelitis, (a severe infection of the bone). He had seen many cases of this whilst he had been treating soldiers from the trenches during World War One.

Given the diagnosis, John's parents were then given the choice of either having John's leg amputated, or allowing an operation to be performed, in which an attempt would be made to drill away the contaminated bone and infection. They opted for the operation.

John subsequently spent the next nine months recovering from the operation with his leg in plaster from the knee down. During this time he had two companions, Arthur Lovett and Ronnie Currington, two other children who were long term patients, in the beds adjacent to him. Arthur had an illness relating to his lungs and unfortunately died. John and Ronnie were never told that he had died, he just disappeared one day and the matter was not discussed. Ronnie had been burnt from his neck to his heels and spent all his period of recovery time on his stomach.

Although this was a children's ward, the parents were only allowed to 'view' their children at 2.30 pm on a Wednesday or Sunday afternoon through slits in the ward doors. Face to face contact was prohibited as it was considered that this would 'unsettle' the children.

The Children's Ward backed on to the Admissions Area of the hospital and was also used as an overflow ward for those who had been admitted with terrific injuries from the bombings. John and his companions frequently witnessed the injured being brought into hospital on stretchers before and after being treated by the doctors. At one point John's consultant thought that just like patients recovering from tuberculosis, John should be kept in his bed outside, all day and all night, only coming back on to the ward for bed baths and treatment. This continued for several months.

After his discharge from hospital John suffered many "flare ups" of the infection and was constantly readmitted. At this time the American doctors based there were trying out an experimental drug called Penicillin. They had been using it on American troops suffering from venereal disease. Although the drug was readily available, the hospital had only very limited access to it. Eventually, it was decided that it should be used in John's treatment. The drug was administered by syringe in the buttocks eight times in a twenty four hour period over several weeks. The drug was then recycled from John's urine by the hospital laboratory where it was refined and then re-injected into him.

The result was the infection was abated and John survived, one of the first civilians in the United Kingdom to be given Penicillin.

Over the next 70 years John has suffered several flare ups of the disease, the last time being during the 1990s, and he is still prescribed Penicillin. Ironically, his daughter is allergic to the drug.

Now, back to the diary.

9th March

Bailly somehow gets me very pleasant meals (middle of the night). This friend of his in the Cook House must have secret resources! The other sisters are complaining about the standard of the meals - I don't comment!

Begin my nights off. Horrid disappointment, Tony doesn't think he will be able to get away.

10th March

Very miserable all day - just about rock bottom when he is announced at 7pm! We depart to our flat in village. Enough said!

11th March

We visit Pompei and the famous ruins.

Start off with a guide and a bag of apples. We have the place to ourselves - not another soul. Our guide hasn't much English and Tony's Italian lends more to the theatre than actual spoken word! Our progress is hilarious. Spent two hours, fantastic place, much of it so beautiful. Also building of 'delights'. I wasn't allowed to see some of these. The guide insisted I stayed outside a certain building, not for innocent female eyes. Tony allowed in, so I made him tell me what I had missed! Hardly mind boggling, I'm not that *innocent! What did impress us was that the 'Ancients' were a jolly sight cleaner than the modern race! Also visited the Cathedral, splendid and overpowering. Over decorated, I thought, gave me a 'funny' feeling - too R.C. (Roman Catholic).*

Salerno club for dinner, then got pulled into a 'party'. Afraid I got a bit pickled. Returned 'home' in very good spirits!

<u>12th March Sunday</u>
Quiet day, lunch in Salerno. Raining hard all day. On duty that night. Tony comes on with me.

13th March
Last twenty four hours together. In a few days Tony goes to Anzio.

14th March
Watch Tony drive off. Very sad, wonder when I shall see him again. Going on duty this evening feeling rather sad, however our weekend was rather fun, and there will be other 'leaves'.

Looking up at Vesuvius it seems a bit livelier, bigger flames, more smoke and strange rumbles!? Bailly doesn't like the look of it but then he never does!

20th March Vesuvius Erupts!!!

7am, Bailly brought my tea. Time to start work. He opens the shutters - black outside. Should be light? Day staff come on, still not getting light. Above, heavy black pall and nasty smell of sulphur! Much speculation, must be Vesuvius, what else? In the Mess, told to "Keep calm, behave as normal".

Night staff to our sleeping quarters, separate building from the Mess, other side of the square. Surprisingly, did go to sleep.

Awakened at 3pm by our batmen with orders from the Colonel to get up, pack a bag with essentials only, and get across to the Mess. The roof of our building in danger of collapse! Shocked to discover that the rather grand steps, twelve I think, leading up to the door, had disappeared under a grey smoking mass of ash and cinders! The level of the square had risen considerably higher, covered in ashes over which we had to walk. We could feel the heat through the soles of our shoes!

Ashes pouring down all day and getting deeper. Roofs collapsing, roads blocked, movement on them impossible. We are completely marooned!

The story of Vesuvius was always my favourite. I never tired of hearing it. With every retelling, she would add a little more detail or give an extra bit of insight. She made it sound so exciting, and enjoyed sharing it.

<u>State of Emergency announced.</u>
However Colonel says we must cope somehow.
A very gloomy Bailly turned up at 8pm to escort me across to the ward. Give him his due, he didn't say "I told you so!"

<u>Nightmare week.</u>
We were cut off for two or three days. Much damage to our buildings. Pioneer Corp. sent to dig us out and clear a route through to the port for our ambulances.

Looking around, what a sight it is - crops ruined, everywhere half buried. Some houses in the village had completely disappeared. Nearer the volcano two villages buried under lava. Took a month for us to get back to normal working. On the second night, some soldiers turned up completely lost.

The Colonel called us all together for an emergency meeting - earthquake likely, following such an enormous eruption - or so the Italian authorities warned. First sign, movement of hanging light fittings, get out of building immediately, not to try and get patients out -no time before collapse of buildings. If uninjured, we are more useful after, helping in rescue work. Shocking but saw the sense of it. Told to tell orderlies the situation. Pray it won't happen.

1st April day duty E1

Been a few staff changes. Meet some new sisters from U.K. They seemed a bit lost, not quite what they expected. They were used to huge wards, long 'rooms' divided into 6 'bays' on each side, 10 beds in each bay - 120 - 3 sisters each ward, 12 orderlies. We share an office and sort out the bays between us, roughly 40 patients each. Told them *they should be pleased they missed the desert if they think this is bad!*

Since going to Anzio I've had lots of letters from Tony but arriving in batches. Post a bit difficult - going the other way too, he says my letters arrive several together. Worrying, I know he is in a very dangerous place. He doesn't say much about it but a lot of wounded coming in here. We now know why we had to have a hospital here in Nocera. It had to be a place close to the small port. Little ships can steal up the coast to Anzio and take the causalities off the landing beaches and slip down again without the Germans noticing - hopefully.

Tony has asked me to look up his Sergeant and a Captain, both admitted two days ago. Managed to find them on E3. Very pleased to see me and full of praise for their Lieut.

I think what impresses me the most was how people took everything in their stride. They simply got on with things even though there was a possibility that death lurked around the corner. Each day could have been their last.

<u>12th April</u>
Supervising serving dinner, fainted. Came round supported by an anxious Bailly - struggled up and assured everyone I was

perfectly alright. Bit groggy though. Retired to the office to gather my wits. Have we hit the jackpot first time?

This appears to be the first mention in the diary of any signs that Mum was potentially pregnant at this time.

<u>17th April</u>
Pretty sure - reported to Major (doctor looking after staff health). He agreed possible pregnancy! He was a bit worried, thought I was too thin, 9st too low for 5ft 9ins. Must take care, said I must come off the wards. Suggests light duties in the Mess.

Very happy, very excited - write letter to Tony. He writes back in the same vane and also saying he feels very proud. Anxious to know what happens next. Had to go to a Medical Board in Naples - seen by a senior doctor there. Everything alright and when safe to travel, shall be posted home end of May. Getting marvelous letters from Tony, trying to get some leave, frantic to see me before I am posted. Sad too that we will be parted for a while.

14th May Sunday

Tony arrives! Flown down from Anzio, very tanned and very dirty! Oh how lovely to see him! Slept out that night at the flat.

15th May Sorrento

Five bitter sweet days. Tony got some transport from H.Q. Everybody being so helpful and kind. Drove into Salerno, then took the scenic route around the coast to Sorrento. Very lovely warm evening with the sun setting behind the mountains, turning them beautiful colours. The sea very calm and blue. Almost dark when we reach the Y.M.C.A. - given sandwiches and coffee. Retire to our own room in the town's major building, large and airy with a little balcony. Stood looking out over this very beautiful romantic town. Spent two more very pleasant days exploring the *town, not doing anything much, just so happy being together.*

We are haunted by the agony of the parting so soon to come though.

Spent a day in Naples. Took the long route around the bay, spectacular views but rather bumpy, damaged road. Did some shopping, lunch at the club, back to Sorrento. Sat on the balcony watching the sun set, listening to Neapolitan music coming from somewhere below. So sad.

<u>*19th May*</u>
Back to the hospital, and Tony leaves to go back to

Anzio. Afraid there were tears, oh so many at this parting. How long will it be before we meet again? Tony thinks not so very long. When the fighting is over in Italy he says the forces will be sent home on much deserved leave and retraining for next move. Must hang onto that thought and look forward. After all, we planned this move - we so badly wanted to start our family, want to be young with our children growing up, we said!

<u>20th May</u>
Transferred to the 104th Base Hospital, to await my journey home to England. Sad farewell to friends,

we've been through a lot together, good and bad times but mostly good on the whole.

Sister's Mess 104th rather splendid villa and very comfortable, great improvement on our barracks at Nocera.

<u>*24th May*</u>
My Birthday. Am 25!
Proceed to docks complete with kit. Board the 'ELNIL', rather battered cargo ship converted to hospital ship. Sail out from Bay of Naples at sundown. Still a lot of damaged ships and wrecks around. Last view of Naples is a mass of twinkling lights.

Home Again

2nd June
Sailed up the Clyde. How green the countryside is!

3rd June
We disembark. Fortunately an orderly to handle my luggage, and got me to the London train. Arrived Euston late evening. Met by mother & sister, (had managed to phone home from Scotland). The city was full of Yanks & all the hotels were booked up. We queued up with everyone else to try and get accommodation. I was dressed in my uniform, the grey and scarlet. One of the officials(?) saw my uniform and took us to the

front of the queue. He managed to find us accommodation.

<u>4th June 1944</u>
Arrive home.

Five months later in November, a baby girl was born, my sister.

Postscript

Tony never saw his daughter. He was due to return to England with Freddie but on 31st July 1945 at 1pm, he died, the day of their second anniversary. It was a bit of a mystery. It might have been pneumonia or something to do with a swimming accident but the facts are not clear. His grave is in Italy along with thousands of other war graves.

And life is Eternal
And Love is Immortal.

What started as a sort of diary to record some events, the biggest adventure of my life, became a love story. The tragic end is not the end, we will be together again.

Part of you Tony, is always

with me as you said it would be, and that part of me that died with you is forever with you, until we meet again, Beloved.

The years have passed. I hardly remember the early post war years. Perhaps I don't want to remember. I struggled to pick up the pieces, make sense of a way of life I hadn't expected. Made numerous mistakes, took forays down several blind alleys! Tried to build a normal life for my daughter who in spite of everything had grown into an adorable and lively little girl.

Although she made a new life for herself, she kept all of Tony's letters. She even kept a couple in her handbag and the handbag went with her wherever she went. I have never read the letters and have no desire to. They belong to my sister now. One day she may read them to gain some understanding of the father that she never knew.

Years later Mum met my father. She called him her knight in shining armour because she felt he had rescued them. She lived a full and happy life and died at the good old age of 94. She died on the very same day as Nelson Mandela. What distinguished company to go out with. She would have liked that!

Acknowledgements

I would like to thank my son Dave for all his hard work and John Hayter for letting me include his story. And thanks to Uncle Freddie.

War Medals